The Longest Day

CELEBRATING THE SUMMER SOLSTICE

BY
Wendy Pfeffer

ILLUSTRATED BY
Linda Bleck

PUFFIN BOOKS
An Imprint of Penguin Group (USA)

PUFFIN BOOKS
Published by the Penguin Group
Penguin Group (USA) LLC
375 Hudson Street
New York, New York 10014

USA ★ Canada ★ UK ★ Ireland ★ Australia
New Zealand ★ India ★ South Africa ★ China

penguin.com
A Penguin Random House Company

First published in the United States of America by Dutton Children's Books,
a division of Penguin Young Readers Group, 2010
Published by Puffin Books, an imprint of Penguin Young Readers Group, 2015

Text copyright © 2010 by Wendy Pfeffer
Illustrations copyright © 2010 by Linda Bleck

Library of Congress Cataloging-in-Publication Data is available upon request.

Puffin Books ISBN 978-0-14-751556-8

Manufactured in China

1 3 5 7 9 10 8 6 4 2

For Milt, who loved long summer days
W. P.

For my husband, David, born on the solstice
L.B.

As summer approaches in the northern part
of the world, bison shed their heavy coats.
Mountain goats climb to sunny pastures,
and with a splash of color
butterflies emerge from silky cocoons.

At this time of year,

the sun appears early each morning, rises higher

into the sky each day, and lingers long into evening.

Days become longer and warmer, and crops grow and ripen.

Families fill playgrounds and parks.

They picnic under an umbrella of green leaves,

play baseball, volleyball, or just nap in the warm sunshine.

Children can ride bikes and play outdoor games for hours

in the evening with the sun *still* in the sky.

FALL (autumnal) EQUINOX
DAY AND NIGHT EQUAL

FALL
nights longer than days

days getting shorter

time to harvest

SUMMER
days longer than nights

days getting shorter

crops grow

WINTER SOLSTICE
THE SHORTEST DAY
WITH THE LEAST SUNSHINE

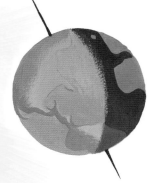

SUMMER SOLSTICE
THE LONGEST DAY
WITH THE MOST SUNSHINE

WINTER
nights longer than days

days getting longer

spring is coming

SPRING
days longer than nights

days getting longer

seedlings sprout

SPRING (vernal) EQUINOX
DAY AND NIGHT EQUAL

Around June 21st, the first day of summer,
as Earth moves in its orbit,
the northern half of the Earth tilts toward the sun
and so it gets more sunshine than the southern half.

The first day of summer,
called the summer solstice,
has more daylight hours
than any other day of the year,
making it the longest day.

The sun, spreading warmth and light,
has always been important to people.
Warm sunshine and more daylight hours
make for a good growing season
to supply life-giving food.

The sun was so valuable to people who lived in ancient times
that some considered it one of their gods.
Egyptians believed their sun god, Ra,
sailed in a golden boat across the sky.

In Mesopotamia, the people imagined their sun god,
Shanash, had a chauffeur drive him across the sky.
Each morning Shanash would come out the "Door of the East,"
and travel across the sky to the "Door of the West."
Then Shanash would travel underground all night
to arrive at the "Door of the East" again in the morning.

The Greeks thought their sun god, Apollo,
drove a chariot through the heavens,
and the sun was one of its blazing wheels.

Early people observed and recorded

how the sun appeared to move through the sky.

They used many methods to chart the sun's path.

Ancient Greeks measured the shadows of a tall pillar.

The shortest shadow occurred on the longest day, in summer,

when the midday sun was high in the sky.

The longest shadow appeared on the shortest day, in winter,

when the midday sun was low in the sky.

The Chumash Indians of California painted a sunburst around
    an opening in the ceiling of a cave.
They called it the House of the Sun. During midafternoon on the
    longest day, the sun's rays streamed through the opening.
When sunlight beamed on a quartz crystal wedged in the ground, the
Chumash Indians welcomed the summer solstice.

Five thousand years ago in England
people began building structures
to mark these special times of the year.
One prehistoric monument, Stonehenge,
consists of a circle of stones.
Some line up with the summer solstice sunrise,
and others line up with the winter solstice sunset.

Over a period of fifteen hundred years,
      workers hauled and rafted
      heavy bluestones and sandstones
      over one hundred miles to Stonehenge.
Some stones were as long as a school bus,
      and weighed fifty tons.
That's heavier than eight large elephants.

Using rollers, ramps, and ropes,
      they set each massive stone in place.
No one knows who these amazing builders were
      or how they moved gigantic stones such long distances,
      but we do know they did it to celebrate the sun.

Similar, yet puzzling, stone structures
cover Mystery Hill in New Hampshire.
Some call it "America's Stonehenge."
While Stonehenge is neatly arranged,
Mystery Hill is a jumble of stones,
many etched with ancient inscriptions.
Some scholars think it was built by an unknown
civilization between 2000 and 5000 years ago.

Early on June 21,

   visitors flock to Mystery Hill.

They watch the sun come up over Sunrise Stone,

   marking the beginning of the longest day.

In Wyoming, during mid-June,
thousands of people hike up Medicine Mountain
to see the Bighorn Medicine Wheel.
Scientists and archaeologists believe the Plains Indians
constructed this eighty-foot-wide circle of rocks
between 200 and 800 years ago.
Twenty-eight spokes radiate out from a central hub.
One spoke points to the summer solstice sunrise,
another to the summer solstice sunset.

Over 700 years ago in Lithuania, villagers celebrated the longest day

by washing their faces with morning dew,

then singing, dancing, and feasting.

They coated a wheel with tar, covered it with straw,

and set it ablaze on top of a hill,

to symbolize the sun at its highest point in the sky.

Then they rolled it down the hill toward a river

to symbolize the sun moving through the sky.

If the wheel was still burning as it hit the water,

they believed the summer sun would produce

a bountiful harvest.

Today Lithuanians and people in many other countries

celebrate St. John's Day on June 24

with festivities from sunup to sundown.

The days around the summer solstice have been called
     Midsummer since long-ago times.
Since June 21 is midway between May and August,
     it is called Midsummer.

On Midsummer Eve, ancient Germanic tribes built fires.
They thought fire would help the sun warm the earth
     and drive away unwanted spirits.
They believed the bigger the fires, the farther away
     those spirits would move.
Couples jumped over the fires hoping that summer crops
     would grow as high as they jumped.

In Bohemia, now known as the Czech Republic,

girls made wreaths with flowers.

Boys collected sticks and branches and built a bonfire.

Girls stood on one side of the blaze and boys on the other.

Each girl held her wreath up and looked through its center

to decide whom she might want to marry.

Then she threw her wreath across the fire to that boy.
They believed the singed wreaths would protect them
against sickness the next year.

On land that lies above the Arctic Circle,

the sun shines for twenty-four hours on June 21.

In Sweden, it is called the day that never ends.

During the Middle Ages on Midsummer Day,

Swedish families decorated houses and barns

with greens to bring good fortune and health.

They stripped branches off a tall spruce tree

and decorated it with garlands of flowers.

Today in Sweden, every town sets up a midsummer pole,
strewn with streamers, flowers, flags, and greens.
Villagers wear folk costumes, play traditional music,
and dance around the pole.
Young people each pick eight different flowers.
They put them under their pillows at night,
hoping to dream about their future spouse.

Each year the people of Nome, Alaska, celebrate

the summer solstice with a Midnight Sun Festival.

On June 21, the sun shines for more than twenty-two hours there.

People parade, barbecue chicken, and dance in the streets.

If the frozen ice is broken up in the Bering Sea, the annual "Polar Bear Swim" is held.

Brave people dip their entire bodies in almost freezing water to celebrate the longest day.

Many people enjoy the heat of summer and outdoor
summertime activities and sports.
On hot summer days children can
wiggle wet toes in squishy sand,
giggle with friends under a sprinkler, and grow
sunflowers that turn slowly all day to keep facing the sun.

At twilight, that time between daylight and darkness,

after the sun sinks below the horizon,

children can gaze at a few bright stars twinkling above

and plan another day of fun in the sun.

During the hot weather, the days shorten
and summer soon ends.
Leaves fall. Cool winds blow.
Bison start growing heavier coats.
Mountain goats wander down to windless pastures,
and monarch butterflies migrate south
to the warm skies of Mexico.

The Earth continues its orbit around the sun
until the next June, when people
in the northern part of the Earth
will once again enjoy the summer solstice
and the longest day of the year.

SOLSTICE FACTS

As the Earth travels around the sun, seasons change because the Earth tilts toward the sun or away from the sun. As the Earth moves in its orbit, the sun appears to move higher and lower in the sky.

The word solstice comes from Latin, where *sol* means "sun," and *sistere* means "stop." A solstice occurs when the sun seems to stop moving away from the equator and starts traveling back toward it.

Around June 21, the North Pole leans toward the sun. The sun's rays, aimed at the Northern Hemisphere, are strong and direct. The sun appears to be high in the sky. It takes it a long time to move from the place where it rises to the place where it sets.

Many hours of sunshine make it the longest day of the year. On that day, the summer solstice, summer begins.

On December 21, the winter solstice, the sun's rays do not shine directly on the Northern Hemisphere. There, the sun appears to be low in the sky.

It takes the sun only a short time to move across the sky, from the place where it rises to the place where it sets. Few hours of sunshine make it the shortest day of the year. On that day, the winter solstice, winter begins.

CREATE YOUR OWN ROCK ART

The Chumash Indians created some of the finest rock art in North America. Much of it depicted people, animals, and the sun, showing the importance of the solstices in their lives. Using these samples from various Chumash rock art paintings, design your own rock art.

What you need:

A smooth, flat stone
Newspaper
Chalk
Acrylic paints (the Chumash used
    red, black, white, and yellow)
Paint brushes of different sizes
(Optional: Matte acrylic sealer)

What to do:

1. After you've found the perfect flat rock, be sure to wash it with water and detergent to remove all the dirt.

2. Let the rock dry inside the house overnight.

3. Spread the newspaper over your work surface.

4. Draw your design first with chalk.

5. Paint over the chalk lines with different colors.

6. Allow the paint to dry for a few hours.

7. You may paint or spray acrylic sealer over the rock to make your rock art last longer.

MAKE A SUNDIAL

The ancient Egyptians used sundials to tell time. Other people designed many types of sundials, sometimes called shadow clocks.

What you need:

A sunny day
Thin cardboard, 6-inch square
Heavy cardboard, 12-inch square
Scissors
Tape
Permanent marker
Compass

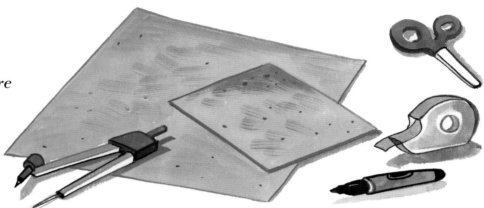

What to do:

1. Fold the corners of your 6-inch square together, then cut along the diagonal crease to make two triangles (see diagram 1). One of these triangles will be your gnomon (no-mon), the part of the sundial that casts a shadow.

2. Fold the bottom inch of the gnomon to make a base (see diagram 2).

3. With your marker, draw a line down the middle of your 12-inch square, making a dot at the center.

4. Stand your gnomon on the square so that it lines up with the marker line and the point of the triangle touches the center dot (see diagram 4).

5. Tape the bottom of the gnomon, allowing it to stand up.

6. Use your compass to find north. Place the sundial in the sun with the high point of the gnomon facing north. Once your sundial is in place, anchor it down with tape or a weight.

7. Each hour of the day, go outside with permanent marker and draw a line where gnomon's shadow falls.

8. Write the hour next to each line (see diagram 5).

9. Go out the next sunny day.

10. If your sundial is in the same place, you can now tell the time by reading the line where the shadow is.

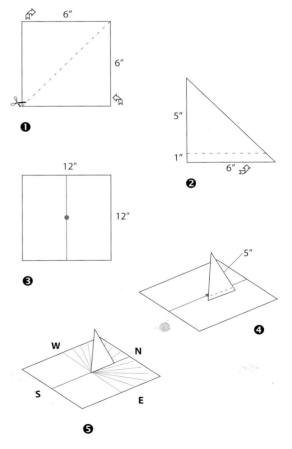

PLANT SUNFLOWERS

Sunflowers are well named because all day long they slowly turn their big heads to face the sun. This head consists of a circle of seeds surrounded by large yellow petals. They are fun to grow.

What you need:

A sunny spot
Rich soil
A packet of seeds (Try helianthus, a giant sunflower.)
A watering can or hose
A stake
String

What to do:

1. Plant the seeds in full summer sun, one inch deep and three feet apart
2. Water the seeds just enough to keep the soil moist.
3. Sunflowers don't need much water or fertilizer.
4. Watch them grow.
5. Measure their height often. Yours could reach three to ten feet tall.
6. Push a stake in the ground next to a seedling of your choice. As your plant grows tie it loosely to the stake.
7. At the end of summer when the petals fall off and the flowers in the center turn black, rub the center with a fork to loosen the black seeds.
8. There may be 1,000 black seeds in the center, so spread them out to dry.
9. Crack open the shell, then enjoy what's inside.
10. You may want to save some for the birds in winter.

MAKE A BOHEMIAN FLOWER WREATH

The Bohemians burned a pinch of the wreath during a thunderstorm to protect them from fire caused by lightning. They also crumbled some of the wreath into their sick animals' food to help heal them.

What you need:

A pail of water
Scissors
A wire coat hanger
Aluminum foil
Floral wire, twine, or strong thread
Brightly colored ribbons
Wildflowers and tall grasses

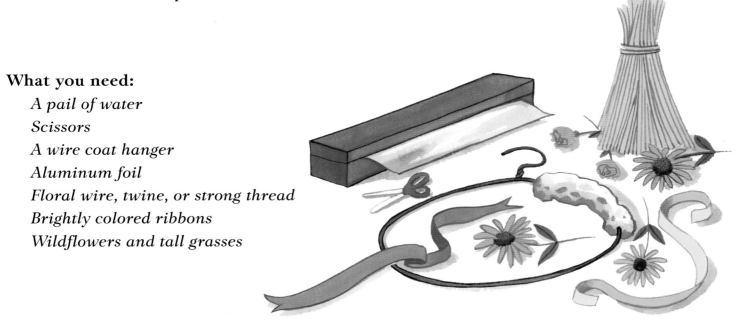

What to do:

1. Collect tall grasses and tie them in bundles with the wire or thread.

2. Hang them up by the thread to dry for about a week.

3. Pick wildflowers, such as Queen Anne's lace, buttercups, clover, and daisies. Do not pull up the roots. You can also find flowers at your local florist or grocery store.

4. Put the flowers in your water pail as you pick them.

5. At home, tie them in bundles and hang them up with thread to dry for a few weeks. A drying rack works perfectly.

6. Stretch the bottom of your coat hanger into a circle, leaving the hook in place.

7. Wrap layers of aluminum foil around the wire to add thickness to your wreath.

8. Wrap the dried grasses over the foil until it's covered.

9. Fasten the grasses with floral wire.

10. Weave the flowers around the wreath and secure them with additional wire.

11. Decorate your wreath with ribbons.

12. Hang it by the coat hanger hook on your door or wall.

FURTHER READING

Jackson, Ellen. *The Summer Solstice.* Brookfield, CT: The Millbrook Press, 2001.

Leslie, Clare Walker. *Nature All Year Long.* New York: Greenwillow Books, 1991.

Markle, Sandra. *Exploring Summer.* New York: Atheneum, 1987.

Milord, Susan. *The Kid's Nature Book.* Charlotte, VT: Williamson Publishing, 1989.

Pfeffer, Wendy. *The Shortest Day: Celebrating the Winter Solstice.* New York: Dutton, 2003.

Pfeffer, Wendy. *We Gather Together: Celebrating the Fall Harvest.* New York: Dutton, 2006.

Pfeffer, Wendy. *A New Beginning: Celebrating the Spring Equinox.* New York: Dutton, 2008

WEBSITES

http://www.factmonster.com/spot/solsticeforkids.html

http://www.chumashindian.com/

http://travelwithkids.about.com/od/familyfunplaces/a/summer solstice.htm

http://www.shrewsburyma.gov/schools/Central/Curriculum/ELEMENTARY/SOCIALSTUDIES/Mesopotamia/ancient mesopotamia.htm

http://www.crystalinks.com/mysteryhill.html